World War I Hero

STUBBY

the Dog Soldier

by BLAKE A. HOENA

illustrated by OLIVER HURST

Content Consultant: Kathy Golden
National Museum of American History, Smithsonian Institution

PICTURE WINDOW BOOKS
a capstone imprint

World War I (1914-1918) was raging across Europe. The Central Powers, led by Germany, had attacked the Allied Powers, which included France, Great Britain, and Russia.

In April of 1917, the United States entered the war, siding with the Allies. Private J. Robert Conroy came to New Haven, Connecticut. He was training in the 102nd Infantry Regiment in the Army's 26th "Yankee" Division.

A young dog was often seen trotting proudly behind Private Conroy. The shabby stray had been shadowing him for weeks, ever since Conroy had tossed the pup a few scraps to eat.

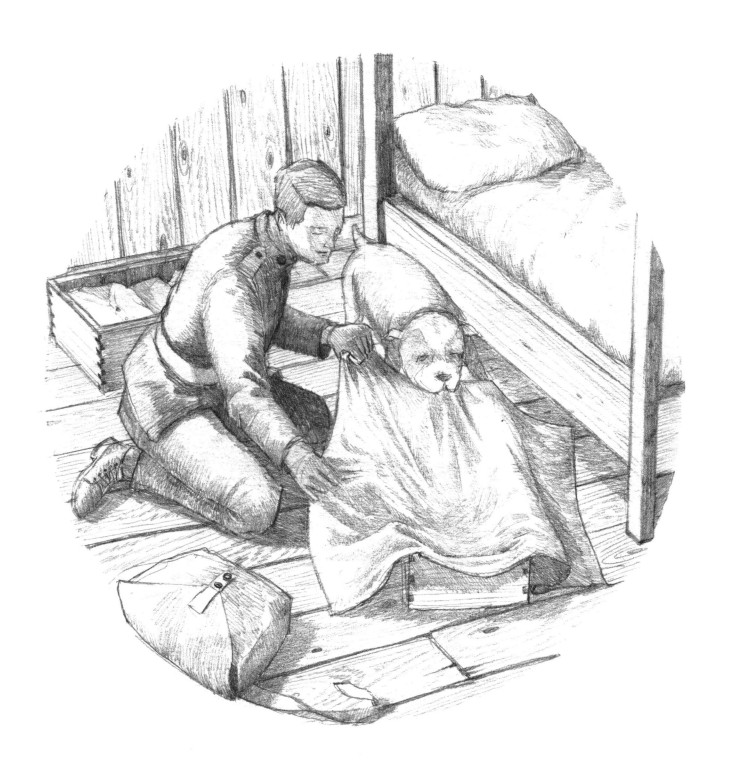

One day Conroy brought his canine friend back to his
barracks. He made a bed for him under his bunk.

The young pup watched as the soldiers talked
excitedly. "Dogs aren't allowed in here!" one said.
Another asked, "What's his name?"

Conroy replied, "Stubby, because of his stubby tail."

Stubby slept in the barracks and ate with
the men. He even took part in training drills.
Conroy trained him to follow commands.

During the summer of 1917, the soldiers of
the 26th headed overseas. They were going
to war. Not wanting to leave Stubby behind,
Conroy snuck him aboard the ship.

After arriving in France, a commanding officer
spotted Stubby. Dogs weren't allowed on the battlefield.
But Stubby was no ordinary pooch. He raised one paw
in salute. The officer was impressed and made
Stubby the "Yankee" Division's mascot.

Soldiers from the 26th were among the first U.S. soldiers to enter the war. What they saw horrified them. The land was torn apart. Lines of injured soldiers were carried off the battlefield.

Early in 1918 the 26th reached the Chemin des Dames. In this dangerous area of France, Stubby and Conroy saw their first action.

They hunkered down in the trenches along
the front line. Bullets whizzed overhead.
Shells thudded nearby. But there was one
danger far more terrifying.

One morning, as the soldiers of the 26th slept, a yellow fog rolled in. It moved west, blowing from enemy lines. The fog drifted across no-man's land and toward their trenches.

Stubby lifted his nose. A deadly scent tainted the air.

Stubby jumped up and ran to the top of the
trench. He barked and howled, trying to wake the
sleeping soldiers. They were exhausted. Gunfire
had kept them up all night.

As Conroy blinked his eyes open, Stubby
darted under a pile of blankets. All that could
be seen of him was his stubby tail.

Then Conroy realized the danger. Mustard gas was
spilling into the trenches. It had been hidden by the
morning fog. "Gas! Gas! Gas!" the cry went out.

Men grabbed respirator masks as poisonous fumes clawed
their lungs. The gas burned their skin and eyes.

Some soldiers suffered from the gas attack.
But no one died. Stubby had saved the day.

And no one would ignore his warnings again.

Stubby quickly grew used to the sounds of war.
And he proved his worth on the battlefield. Darting about,
he yipped encouragement to his fellow soldiers.

If a soldier got hurt in battle, Stubby dashed
to his side. He then barked to alert medics so they
could find the wounded man.

Slowly the Allies pushed back the Germans.
In July of 1918, the fighting moved to the small
town of Chateau Thierry.

The battle was deadly. Stubby and the 26th
crawled forward through bomb craters. They ducked
under sniper fire.

Suddenly Stubby's ears perked up. He heard a
mortar shell whistling toward them. Stubby dropped
to the ground just before the bomb exploded.

With Stubby's cues, the soldiers knew when to take
cover because of an approaching bomb.

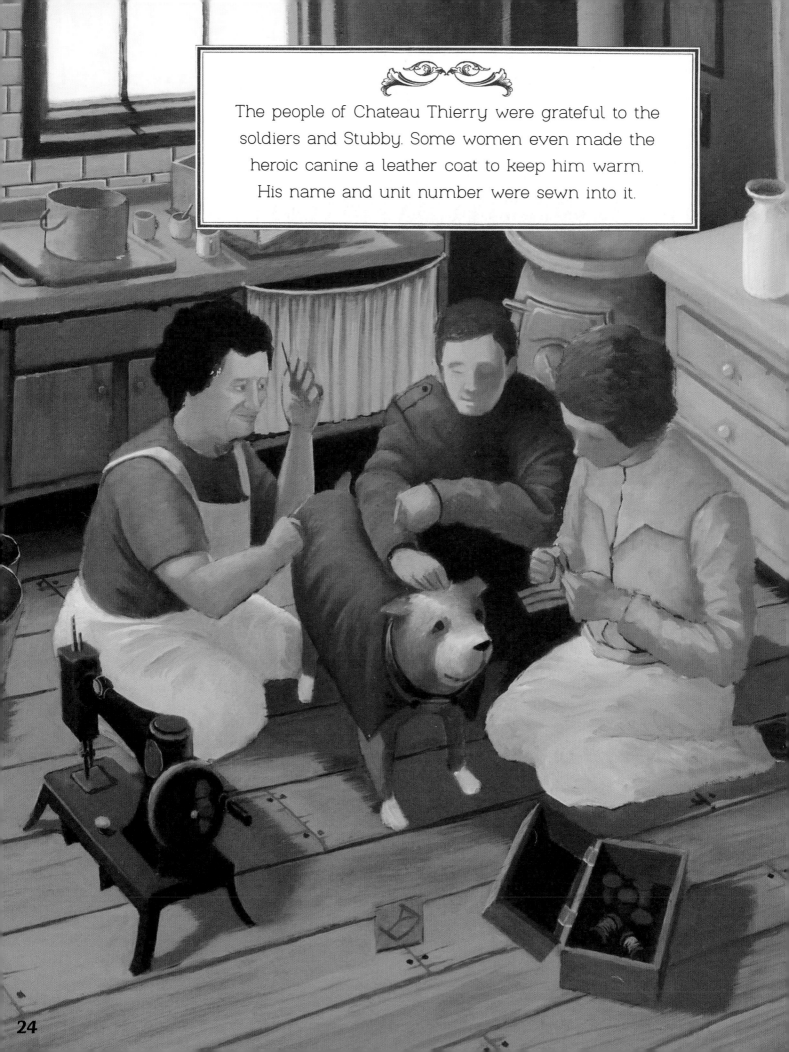

The people of Chateau Thierry were grateful to the soldiers and Stubby. Some women even made the heroic canine a leather coat to keep him warm. His name and unit number were sewn into it.

Stubby's duties didn't end there. One morning,
as the soldiers snored and grunted in their sleep, a dark
shadow crept through no-man's land. Stubby's ears
perked up. His nose twitched.

Stubby's growls jarred Conroy awake. The soldier grabbed his rifle, fearing an attack. He peeked over the top of the trench. A German soldier lay face down in the mud. Stubby stood on his back.

The growling Stubby had a hold of the enemy's trousers.
He wouldn't let go until his fellow soldiers took the German
prisoner. From then on he became known as "*Sergeant* Stubby."

On November 11, 1918, the Central Powers surrendered to the Allies. Shortly afterward Private Conroy again snuck Stubby aboard ship. But this time, to return home.

Afterword

Stubby was treated like a true hero. He marched in parades and was awarded a gold medal for his bravery. But his story didn't end with the war. Conroy enrolled at Georgetown University, where he would study law. Stubby joined him on campus and charmed his way into becoming the football team's mascot. He even performed during half-time shows.

In 1926 Stubby passed away. His body can be seen on display at the National Museum of American History, Smithsonian Institution.

Today the United States has military dog training programs. Dogs serve bravely in conflicts around the world. They sniff out bombs and other dangers for the soldiers they work with.

Glossary

Allied Powers-the victors in World War I, which included France, the United Kingdom, and the United States

artillery-large guns, like a cannon

barracks-a building where soldiers are housed

Central Powers-the aggressors in World War I, which included Germany, Austria-Hungary, and the Ottoman Empire

commanding officer-the person in charge of a military unit

mascot-a person or thing that is used to represent a group or team

mustard gas-a poisonous gas used mostly during World War I; mustard gas damages the lungs if breathed in and burns exposed skin

no-man's land-the area between enemy trenches where most of the fighting (and dying) took place during World War I

respirator mask-a mask worn over the nose and mouth; a respirator masks stops poisonous fumes from being breathed in

sniper-a soldier trained to shoot people from a hidden place

stray-a homeless animal, such as a lost or abandoned dog or cat

Read More

Gagne, Tammy. *Military Dogs*. Dogs on the Job. North Mankato, Minn.: Capstone Press, 2013.

Goldish, Meish. *Soldiers' Dogs*. Dog Heroes. New York: Bearport Publishing, 2013.

Patent, Dorothy Hinshaw. *Dogs on Duty: Soldiers' Best Friends on the Battlefield and Beyond*. New York: Walker & Co., 2012.

Critical Thinking Using the Common Core

Private Conroy was lucky to have Stubby as a companion during their adventures. During World War I, the United States military did not have a dog-training program, and dogs weren't typically allowed in camp or on ships. How might this story be different for Conroy if he did not have Stubby by his side? *(Key Ideas and Details)*

Thinking back on Stubby's tale, re-read the introduction. Were there clues in the introduction that gave you hints to what would happen in the story? *(Craft and Structure)*

Stubby was just one of many heroic animals throughout history. Look online to find stories about other dogs that served in the military. How do their stories differ from Stubby's? How are they the same? *(Integration of Knowledge and Ideas)*

Internet Sites

FactHound offers a safe, fun way to find Internet sites related to this book. All of the sites on FactHound have been researched by our staff.

Here's all you do:

Visit *www.facthound.com*

Type in this code: 9781479554614

Super-cool stuff! Check out projects, games and lots more at **www.capstonekids.com**

Editor: Jeni Wittrock
Designer: Ashlee Suker
Art Director: Nathan Gassman
Production Specialist: Tori Abraham
The illustrations in this book were created with oils on board and pencil.

Picture Window Books are published by Capstone,
1710 Roe Crest Drive, North Mankato, Minnesota 56003
www.capstonepub.com

Library of Congress Cataloging-in-Publication Data
Hoena, B. A.
Stubby the Dog Soldier: World War I Hero/by Blake Hoena; illustrated by Oliver Hurst.
pages cm.—(Nonfiction Picture Books. Animal Heroes)
Includes bibliographical references.
Summary: "Simple text and full-color illustrations describe the true story of Stubby the
World War I dog"—Provided by publisher.
Audience: Grades K–3.
ISBN 978-1-4795-5461-4 (hardcover)
ISBN 978-1-4795-5465-2 (paperback)
ISBN 978-1-4795-5759-2 (paper over board)
ISBN 978-1-4795-5469-0 (ebook pdf)
1. Stubby (Dog)—Juvenile literature. 2. World War, 1914–1918—Dogs—Juvenile literature.
3. Dogs—War use—United States—History—20th century—Juvenile literature. I. Title.
D639.D6H64 2015
940.4'12730929—dc23   2014011344

Photo Credit: Corbis/Bettmann, 29

Printed in the United States of America in North Mankato, Minnesota
032014   008087CGF14

Look for all the books in the series:

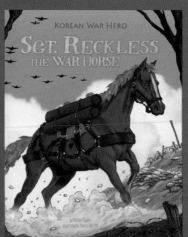
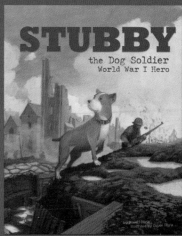